Simply Science

Marvellous MATERIALS

Steve Way

Illustrations: Steve Boulter & Xact Studio

Diagrams: Karen Radford

AUTHOR: **STEVE WAY**
EDITOR: **FELICIA LAW**
ILLUSTRATORS:

         STEVE BOULTER
         XACT STUDIO
DESIGN: **RALPH PITCHFORD**

Copyright © 2008 Diverta Limited
All rights reserved

ISBN 978-1-906292-14-0
Printed in China

PHOTO CREDITS:

p.5 Avner Richard/Shutterstock Inc.
p.8 Garden World Images.
p.8-9 ARTEKI/Shutterstock Inc.
p.9 (cr)Darko Novakovic/Shutterstock Inc.,
(b) Mike Norton/Shutterstock Inc.
p.10 (cl) George Roos/Peter Arnold Inc/Science Photo
Library, (c) Charles Taylor/Shutterstock Inc., (cr) Shang
Pei Lin/Shutterstock Inc.,(br) Zsolt Horvath/Shutterstock Inc.
p.11 (l) Vladimir Korostyshevskiy/Shutterstock Inc.,
(r) Dario Diament/Shutterstock Inc.
p.12 David Hughes/Shutterstock Inc.
p.13 Silas Lindenstein/Shutterstock Inc.
p.15 Phil Degginger/Stone Collection/Getty Images.
p.16 R. Maisonneuve, PUBLIPHOTO DIFFUSION/Science
Photo Library.
p.17 (tl) Chris McCooey/Shutterstock Inc., (tc) Paul Butchard/
Shutterstock Inc., (tr) J. Helgason/Shutterstock Inc.
p.18 (bl) Jostein Hauge/Shutterstock Inc.,
(cr) O'Jay R. Barbee/Shutterstock Inc.
p.19 (tl) Gail Johnson/Shutterstock Inc.,
(br) TAOLMOR/Shutterstock Inc.
p.20 Fritz Goro/Time & Life Pictures/Getty Images.
p.21 Ozkan Uner/Shutterstock Inc.
p.22 - 23 Trout55/Shutterstock Inc.
p.23 Aiti/Shutterstock Inc.
p.25 (l) Isidora Milic/Shutterstock Inc.,
(r) Mike Liu/Shutterstock Inc.
p.26 (bl) Nick Stubbs/Shutterstock Inc.,
(tr) Antonio Iacovelli/Shutterstock Inc.
p.27 (tr) Joanne Harris and Daniel Bubnich/Shutterstock Inc.,
(b) Car Photo Library.

Cover
Phil Degginger/Stone Collection/Getty Images.

Marvellous MATERIALS

Contents

What are materials?

It may sound confusing, but materials are the things we use to make all the things we use! For example, wood, stone and metals are all materials. We use metals to make cars, planes, boats, buildings, wires, and even cutlery!

Sometimes a single material is used to help us in some way. For example, we can make clothes out of wool, and cotton materials. Sometimes several materials are combined to make a mixture; for example, when metal and rubber are combined to make a strong wheel.

Materials can be ...

solid ... like bricks, metals and plastics

or **liquid** ... like dyes, inks and paints

or **gases** ... like oxygen and hydrogen for fuel, or neon for lights ...

All kinds of sturdy materials have been used to construct the things you can see in this photo.

Plants have always been useful to people, not only as a source of food but also of useful materials. One of the most useful materials we get from plants is wood.

We needed wood as a material to help us use one of our greatest ever inventions – fire! Wood fires didn't just help people stay warm and protect homes from dangerous animals, often fire was used for hunting!

Even huge animals like woolly mammoths could be scared by people brandishing fire brands – so scared they could be chased to the edges of hills and cliffs. When the mammoths fell off the cliff it was time to have a feast!

Some scientists think that humans hunted so successfully with fire and spears that we might have hunted the woolly mammoths into extinction.

Wood has been used for building for thousands of years as it is such a strong material. Amazingly, when used in certain ways, wood can be four to five times stronger than steel!

Because it floats on water, wood has always been made into boats and rafts of all shapes and sizes.

Wood has also been used for making furniture, vehicles and machines.

Viking longships, which were the fastest sailing ships of their day, were so highly prized that kings were buried in their ships!

Growing wood

Trees take in water from the soil through their roots. The water travels up the tree through hollow, woody tubes and is carried to the leaves. The trees have to make new tubes each year because they stop working after this time. That's why trees gradually grow wider and wider – and produce lots of useful wood!

Trees are also a source of food as they produce fruits like apples, mangoes, bananas and nuts like walnuts and brazil nuts.

Plants have also been used in medicine for thousands of years. Even the modern drug, aspirin, comes from a substance found in the bark of willow trees.

How old is the tree?

A tree's growth varies from year to year depending on the weather. Scientists can count the rings of woody tubes in the trunk to work out how old a tree is! Some trees are thousands of years old!

age rings

Bananas give us energy to work and play!

Bristlecone pines from the Rocky Mountains in the USA are some of the longest living trees.

Rock

One of the first materials available to people were the many different kinds of rock they found around them. Many early weapons, for example, were made from a rock called flint because it's very hard and strong.

So what kinds of rock are there? Well our Earth holds hundreds of different kinds of rock, but there are three main types and these are made in different ways.

1. Igneous rock

Only a few kilometres underneath the hard rock we all live on, the rock is so hot it's melted, or molten! When that molten rock is pushed up to the surface – for example when a volcano erupts – it flows out as lava which cools down and turns into solid rock. These kind of rocks are called igneous rocks.

Basalt and granite

Basalt rocks and granite are two common types of igneous rock.

2. Sedimentary rock

Have you ever poured sand or soil into a bucket of water? All the material that finally settles on the bottom of the bucket is known as 'sediment'. Sedimentary rock was made from rocks, stones and other materials that settled in layers, usually under the sea. More and more layers piled up on top, pressing the bottom layers into hard rock.

Limestone

Limestone is a type of sedimentary rock often used in buildings and statues. Limestone rocks sometimes contain the shells of prehistoric sea creatures that sank to the bottom of the sea when they died!

3. Metamorphic rock

These rocks are formed from other types of rock that have been changed because they've been ground to a powder by huge stresses and pressures or heated up to very high temperatures.

Marble

Marble is a type of metamorphic rock formed from ground up or heater limestone.

The beautiful Taj Mahal in Agra, India, is made from marble!

Useful rocks

Stone is very hard wearing but can be chiselled, carved and even smashed into all sorts of shapes. For this reason, stone has been used since ancient times for making special buildings, such as monuments.

The pyramids of Egypt, and the Mayan and Aztec temples in South America, have survived to today because they were made of stone. Another famous ancient stone monument is Stonehenge in England. The construction of Stonehenge began over 5,000 years ago. As the builders didn't have metal tools, they used pointed deer antlers to dig holes in the ground and then put the gigantic stones in. Some of the stones they used weigh 25 tonnes!

Bits of rock

The soil that plants grow in is mainly made up of tiny fragments of rock and stone. They provide valuable minerals and a base for the plants to grow in. As dead plant material, called humus, builds up in the soil it becomes more fertile.

Perhaps Stonehenge
was built as a
gigantic calendar.
It may also have been
used as a primitive
laboratory to study
the stars, and even
as a tool to work
out how big the
Earth was!

13

Metals

Over five thousand years ago, people began to find a useful material – metal – inside the rocks around them.

Sometimes the metal was found in a pure form. Usually, however, it was found scattered in bits of rock and minerals. The rocks had to be broken up and heated so the molten metal could be picked out.

Making a pure metal

1. One of the first metals to be used was copper. A thousand years later, people found they could mix the copper with another metal called tin to make bronze.

2. The bronze weapons and tools people made were even better and stronger than the stone tools they'd been using. Bronze was far easier to shape into different forms than stone!

3. After about another 1,000 years, people realised they could make many more things out of a metal called iron. There was lots of it about.

Making iron

These days iron is purified in an enormous 'blast furnace' so that tonnes of iron can be purified each time it is used.

Steel can be made from iron by adding a small amount of coke to the iron. Steel can be even more useful for making things than iron, as it doesn't rust so easily.

A modern blast furnace.

4. The trouble was that the iron was all mixed up with the minerals, or iron ore, they found it in. They needed to get it out as pure iron - to 'purify' it.

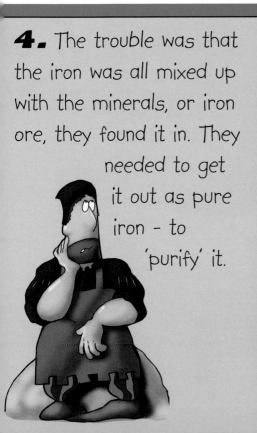

5. But first they needed to heat the iron to a very high temperature.

6. They then added charcoal, made from wood or coal, to the mix. This helped purify the iron ore so that they could make pure iron!

Paper

When computers came along, everyone thought that offices would become 'paperless offices' and that books would disappear. Well, even though computers are very useful, offices still use lots of paper, and more and more books are being made. Paper is such an amazingly useful material!

Rag paper

Surprisingly, it's only recently – since the 1800s – that paper has mainly been made from wood. Since the first paper was made over 2,000 years ago, most of it has been made from old rags! In fact, just before wood began to be used there was a shortage of old rags! Today, some special types of paper are still made from rags!

Cutting down trees

Because paper is mostly made from wood, lots of trees are being cut down to supply it. It's very important to 're-cycle' as much paper as we can – and old paper can be mashed into pulp just like wood can.

Paper can be mashed into pulp over and over again, so we are able to recycle it easily.

Origami

Origami is the name for the art of paper folding that originated in Japan. The paper has to be folded into elaborate shapes without being cut, pasted or decorated.

Papier mache

The art of mixing paper with paste or glue so it can be moulded into all sorts of shapes originated in oriental countries hundreds of years before it spread to Europe in the 1700s.

Wallpaper

Patterned paper was first used to decorate walls sometime in the 1400s. To begin with, it was hand-painted so very expensive. Now it can be made much more cheaply.

So how is paper made?

Paper is usually made from mashed up wood pulp. But in the past, mashed up rags were used instead. Some paper can be made from other plants like sugar cane, straw and flax.

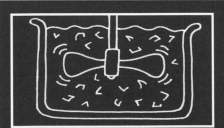

1. Firstly the wood is mashed up into a pulp with lots of water. That makes the fibres in the wood separate and swell up.

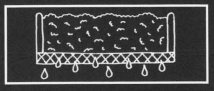

2. Then, excess water is filtered off and the pulp is formed into a sheet.

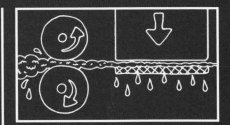

3. The wet sheet of pulp is pressed very tightly to push out even more water. Modern paper mills do this by pressing the sheet between rollers.

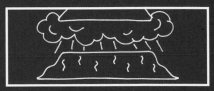

4. Finally, the sheet is dried. The fibres stick to each other to make paper!

Natural fabrics

Many materials are made into fabrics. Fabrics have always been important because we need them to make clothes as well as other things in our homes. Carpets, coverings for furniture and curtains are all made from fabric.

Some of the materials we use come from the plants and animals around us. We call these natural fabrics.

Cotton

Cotton is grown all over the world. It comes from a flowering shrubby plant. Once it has flowered, it leaves small green seedpods, which are called 'cotton bolls'. These have the seeds of the plant inside them. Cotton is made from the fibres that grows inside the pods. This can be picked out of the ripe cotton bolls by hand or by machine. The fibres are made into thread.

Linen

Linen is made from the fibres of a flowering plant called flax. It is very strong and durable and can be used to make light clothes and tough canvas bags and tents. Linen is one of the oldest materials made by people. Archaeologists have found that prehistoric peoples used linen in Switzerland and linen fabrics have also been found in Ancient Egyptian tombs.

Silk

Silk is made by moth caterpillars, called silk worms. The caterpillars produce a silky fibre that comes out of their heads and which they wrap around themselves to make their cocoon. Silk is made from this long fibre. Silk-making began thousands of years ago in China and spread to India and Japan. The silk industry didn't begin in Europe until two Persian monks smuggled some silk worms out of China that they hid inside hollow bamboo canes!

Wool

Wool is made from the furry coats, or fleece, of sheep, goats and camels. The best fleeces are shaved, or sheared, from the animals in the warm weather so they can grow a new one before the following winter. Wool has lots of air-spaces in it that traps heat. Amazingly, it also slowly absorbs moisture from cold, damp air as it's being worn. This makes it warmer to wear.

Man-made fabrics

The first man-made fibres tried to copy natural materials. When scientists wanted to invent a chemical version of silk, they came up with rayon, a fibre made from a chemical called cellulose which is found in wood from trees. Since then, scientists have invented more and more clever fabrics.

Spandex is made from fibres of plastic called polyurethane. The amazing thing about Spandex fibres is that they can be stretched without breaking – up to five or six times their original length. For this reason Spandex is used to make flexible sportswear like swimsuits, running and cycling clothes.

Lycra Lycra is a very popular form of Spandex worn by athletes such as cyclists.

Rayon

Rayon is made by forcing wood cellulose, and the chemicals mixed with it, through a nozzle with tiny holes in it. The chemicals come out of the tiny holes as rayon fibres. Viscose rayon, the most popular rayon, is used to make things like clothes and underwear, carpets and surgical materials.

Nylon was invented in the 1930s in the USA, and was often made in the same way as rayon. Nylon is a plastic that can be moulded into solid shapes. It is very strong and bendy and was used at first to make clothes, particularly women's stockings. Then, when World War II started, the new material was also used to make parachutes and towlines. Nylon can also be made into the bristles on your toothbrush.

Velcro imitates a plant called burdock. Its seeds have hooked heads that stick to people and animals that pass by. Velcro is made from two pieces of nylon fabric that stick together when they touch - useful for fastening sports shoes, for example.

In the future...

Scientists are planning to make all kinds of new materials in the future. Already a tough resin called Teflon that was first used to make non-stick saucepans is being used to make non-rip trousers.

Scientists are adding tiny chemicals (and maybe bacteria) to fabrics to make them self-cleaning! The chemicals and bacteria will be able to break up the dirt and perspiration. You'll be able to wear clothes for longer without having to wash them!

Some fabrics may contain heat-sensitive electronics which will be able to tell a computer how well a person is and where they are. These may help people doing dangerous jobs, like fire-fighters and people who do high risk sports.

Liquids

Many materials like wood and metals are hard and strong, so it's easy to see why they're called 'solids'. Other materials are soft and bendy like fabrics, but they're also called solids. So what's the difference between a solid material and a liquid material?

All materials are made of very very tiny particles called atoms, most of which are joined in tiny groups called molecules.

In a 'solid' material the atoms or molecules can't move around very much, they just vibrate from side to side. So when you place a solid in different containers, it still stays the same shape.

In a liquid, all the atoms or molecules can move around each other, so the liquid changes shape easily. If you pour a liquid into different containers, it will become the shape of the container it is in.

Wonderful water

What's so special about water? Well for a start, life on Earth couldn't exist without it. Water has all sorts of useful properties that help keep us alive and make it the most useful material we use.

1. Water is a good solvent. Other materials can 'dissolve' in, which means that they can become mixed in with the water.

2. Water can form an emulsion. If some materials don't completely dissolve in it, they can still float around in it as an emulsion. Milk, salad creams and some paints are emulsions.

3. Water can absorb a lot of energy. What this means is that it takes a lot of energy to heat water up but also that water has to lose a lot of energy before it cools again.

Rubber

Rubber is the fluid that drips from rubber trees. When it dries, it becomes solid. In 1839 Charles Goodyear found that if he mixed rubber with sulphur and heated it, it became much stronger. It could be used for making car and bicycle tyres.

Most of the rubber we use today is made from 'synthetic' rubber using chemicals. However, natural rubber is still used to make tyres for racing cars, trucks, buses and aeroplanes.

Liquid rubber is caught in a cup.

Gases

Gases contain parts called molecules, just like liquids do. These move about all over the place, bumping into each other from time to time! Several gases are very useful materials.

Oxygen

Oxygen is a useful gas because it's the gas we breathe to keep us alive! Oxygen helps things burn more easily and so oxygen is often mixed with fuels in rocket engines, for example, to make them burn better. You can usually put out a fire by smothering it in some way so it stops the oxygen getting to the flames.

Many rockets are powered by oxygen and hydrogen gases.

Hydrogen

Hydrogen is another very useful gas. Most of the Sun is made up of hydrogen. The energy it gives off is what produces the light and heat that make life on Earth possible!

Many scientists believe that hydrogen will be the fuel of the future. This is because when it's burned, it only produces water instead of the gases produced by burning hydrocarbons.

Unfortunately, using hydrogen isn't always safe. As it is lighter than normal air, hydrogen was once used to fill airships. But then a terrible disaster happened when the hydrogen in the large airship, Hindenburg, burst into flames and many people were killed. Beacuse of this, airships are no longer used to carry passengers.

Nitrogen

Nitrogen is another useful gas! The air is mostly made up of nitrogen. Nitrogen is taken out of the air by tiny bacteria living in the soil and in the roots of certain plants. This helps the plants make proteins that human beings need to eat to stay alive!

Steam

Steam is the gas form of water. Most gases take up a lot more space when they change from being a liquid to a gas. This is what happens with steam when it is heated in a container. As it expands, it presses against the sides of the container.

When the pressure is released, it forms energy that can be used to power steam engines or to spin the turbines in a power station and make electricity.

Neon

Neon is one of a family of gases called 'Noble Gases'. They were called that because they seemed too 'noble' to react with other chemicals. The exciting thing about neon and other similar gases is that when an electric current is passed through them, they are made to glow in different colours.

Neon is used in the neon lights that make city lights look so exciting!

Glass

What do you think you could make from this sandy beach other than a sandcastle? Well, if you heat up sand to a very high temperature, about 1,700 degrees Centigrade, you can make it into a very useful material – glass!

Stained-glass windows make buildings much more interesting and beautiful to look at.

Because it's very expensive to heat sand to a high temperature, another substance called soda is usually added. You only have to heat the mixture to 850 degrees centigrade – but that's still very hot!

The glass that's made from sand and soda is called water glass – and it dissolves in water! So a little lime, made from limestone, must also be added to make normal glass. Metals can also be added to colour the glass.

Optic fibres

In modern times we have been able to make long, thin fibres of glass, called optic fibres. They're called this because you can send light along them. Computer data, voices and pictures can all be changed into pulses of light that travel along fibres.

Light travels along the fibres by reflecting against the sides. They can also be used in medicine to see inside the body.

Fibreglass

Glass can be made into fibres that are then formed into a kind of glass 'wool', or moulded into a solid shape. Fibre glass wool is good at cutting out sound and keeping in heat, so it's often used as insulation in buildings. Fibreglass is also used to make car bodies and small boats.

Marcos Mantis GT – its fibre-glass body looks great!

Materials together

There are many useful ways in which two or more materials can work together.

A thermometer, for example is an instrument for measuring temperature. It uses three materials, glass, air and metal.

Hot or cold?

One heat-measuring scale is called the Fahrenheit scale after the scientist who invented it. But today we mostly use the Celsius scale to measure temperature. 0 degrees is the freezing point of pure water and 100 degrees is its boiling point.

1. People have always known whether things were hot or cold. They could feel the difference!

2. But until the 1700s there was no way of telling exactly what the temperature was. There were only inaccurate gadgets that helped record temperature using warm air or alcohol.

3. A scientist called Gabriel Fahrenheit decided to try and invent an accurate thermometer.

4. He used a metal called mercury that expanded as it became hotter and rose up the tube. He needed to mark the thermometer with a scale to read off how the mercury had risen.

5. Gabriel Fahrenheit marked his mercury tube at the exact temperature at which salt water froze – 32 degrees. Then he continued to mark the scale upwards and finished it at 212 degrees – the point at which water boils. We still use this scale today.

Materials Quiz

1. What type of rocks form after a volcano has erupted?

_____

2. What metal did prehistoric people make from mixing copper and tin?

_____

3. How heavy were some of the stones used to build Stonehenge?

_____

4. Where could Viking kings be buried?

_____

5. What was paper mainly made from before wood was used?

1. Igneous. 2. Bronze. 3. 25 tonnes 4. In their longships 5. Rags 6. Moth (caterpillars) 7. Rayon 8. Water 9. Hydrogen 10. Glass

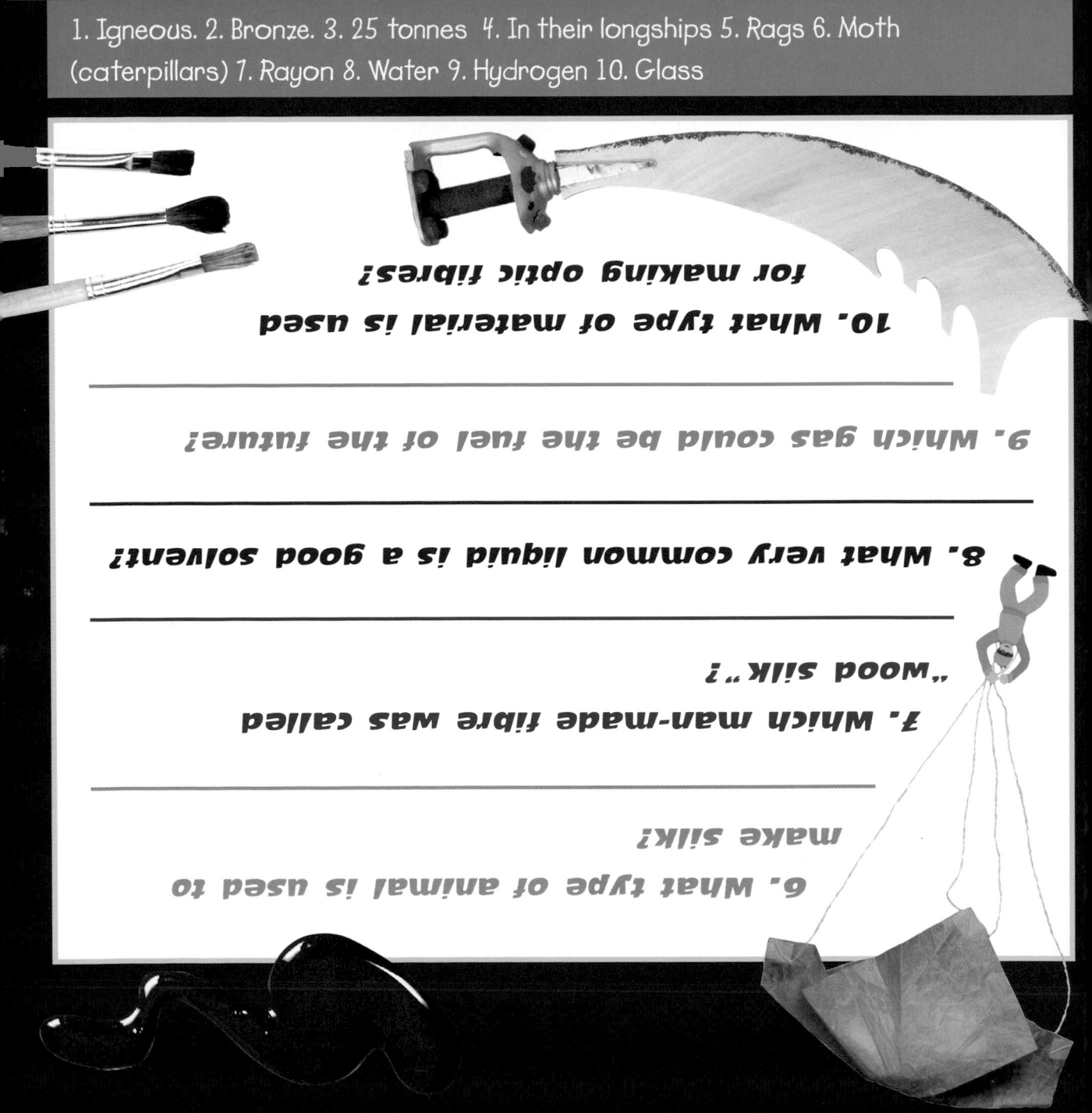

6. What type of animal is used to make silk?

7. Which man-made fibre was called "wood silk"?

8. What very common liquid is a good solvent?

9. Which gas could be the fuel of the future?

10. What type of material is used for making optic fibres?

Index